SHARK ATTACK!

By Cathy East Dubowski

Penguin
Random
House

Series Editor Deborah Lock
Project Editors Caryn Jenner, Carey Combe
Editor Rohini Deb
US Editors Regina Kahney, Shannon Beatty
Senior Art Editor Ann Cannings
Art Editors Karen Lieberman, Kanika Kalra
Senior Producer, Pre-production Ben Marcus
Picture Researchers Jamie Robinson, Sumedha Chopra
Illustrators Malcolm McGregor, Peter Dennis
Jacket Designer Charlotte Jennings
DTP Designer Anita Yadav
Managing Editor Soma B. Chowdhury
Managing Art Editor Ahlawat Gunjan
Publishing Manager Bridget Giles

Reading Consultant
Linda Gambrell, Ph.D.

First American Edition, 1998
Other editions, 2009
This edition, 2015
Published in the United States by DK Publishing
345 Hudson Street, New York, New York 10014

Copyright © 1998, 2009, 2015 Dorling Kindersley Limited
DK, a Division of Penguin Random House LLC
17 18 19 10 9 8 7 6 5 4
004—271722—Sept/15

A catalog record for this book is available
from the Library of Congress.

ISBN: 978-1-4654-3506-4 (Paperback)
ISBN: 978-1-4654-3507-1 (Hardcover)

DK books are available at special discounts when purchased in bulk for sales promotions, premiums, fund-raising, or educational use. For details, contact:
DK Publishing Special Markets
345 Hudson Street, New York, New York 10014
SpecialSales@dk.com

Printed and bound in China

The publisher would like to thank the following for their kind permission to reproduce their photographs:
(Key: a=above, b=below/bottom, c=center, l=left, r=right, t=top)

7 **Ardea London:** P. Morris (b). 10 **Planet Earth Pictures:** Marty Snyderman (b). 11 **Ardea London:** Ron & Valerie Taylor (cl). 12 **Ardea London:** Ron & Valerie Taylor (b). 13 **Ardea London:** Kev Deacon (t). 14 **Getty Images:** Reinhard Dirscherl (b). 15 **Getty Images:** Stephen Frink (t). 16 **The Ronald Grant Archive:** Jaws: The Revenge, 1987 © MCA / Universal Pictures (bl). **Mary Evans Picture Library:** (br). 17 **Ardea London:** Ron & Valerie Taylor (cl). **Planet Earth Pictures:** Norbert Wu (cr); Doug Perrine (b). 20 **Ardea London:** Ron & Valerie Taylor (br). 21 **Ardea London:** D. Parer & E. Parer-Cook (tl); Ron & Valerie Taylor (tr); Adrian Warren (b). 26 **Getty Images:** Luis Javier Sandoval (bl). **Corbis:** Fred Bavendam / Minden Pictures (br). 27 **SuperStock:** Norbert Wu (bl). 123RF.com: Fiona Ayerst (br). 28 **Ardea London:** Ron & Valerie Taylor (t). **Innerspace Visions:** Bob Cranston (br). 31 **Planet Earth Pictures:** F.J. Jackson (b). 32 **Planet Earth Pictures:** Doug Perrine (t). **Ardea London:** Ron & Valerie Taylor (b). 33 **Ardea London:** Ron & Valerie Taylor (cl). 35 **Wild Images:** Howard Hall (b). 36 **Corbis:** National Geographic Creative (cl). **Getty Images:** Roland Birke (br). 37 **Dorling Kindersley:** David Peart / David Peart (br). **Getty Images:** Watt Jim (tr). 39 **Smithsonian Institution, NMNH:** Chip Clark. 43 **Oxford Scientific films:** Richard Herrmann (cl). **Ardea London:** Ron & Valerie Taylor (br). 44 **Ardea London:** Ron & Valerie Taylor (c). **T. Britt Griswold:** (bl) 44–45 **Planet Earth Pictures:** James D. Watt (b). 46 **naturepl.com:** Jurgen Freund (t). 47 **Alamy Images:** Jurgen Freund / Nature Picture Library (br). **SuperStock:** Minden Pictures (tl). 48 **Ardea London:** Ron & Valerie Taylor (tr). **Innerspace Vision:** Nigel Marsh (bl). 49 **Pictor International:** (tr). **Innerspace Visions:** Kurt Amsler (b). 50 **Planet Earth Pictures:** Doug Perrine (cl). 52 **Science Photo Library:** BSIP LECA (tl). 53 **Waterhouse stock Photography:** Stephen Frink (br). 54 **Innerspace Visions:** Doug Perrine (t). 55 **Planet Earth Pictures:** James D. Watt (b).
Jackets: Front: Corbis: Mike Parry / Minden Pictures. iStockphoto.com: Benguhan cb. **Back: Corbis:** Marty Snyderman t.

All other images © Dorling Kindersley
For further information see: www.dkimages.com

A WORLD OF IDEAS:
SEE ALL THERE IS TO KNOW

www.dk.com

Contents

Shark Attack!

Rodney Fox had almost run out of time. He needed to find a big fish— and he needed to find it soon. The young Australian was competing in an annual spearfishing championship. To win he had to find and catch a big local fish. Rodney had won the contest last year, and he wanted to win again. But today something would happen. Something that would change his life forever.

Like all the other competitors in the contest, Rodney wore a line fixed to his dive belt to hold the fish he had caught. He and the other divers had been diving for several hours. They had caught a lot of fish, and the water smelled of blood.

About half a mile (1 km) offshore, Rodney spotted a huge morwong—just the fish he needed to win! Carefully, he aimed his spear gun at the fish.

CRASH! Something slammed hard into Rodney's side. He felt as if he had been hit by an express train!

It was a great white shark! The force of the impact knocked the mask off his face and the spear gun from his hand. His left shoulder disappeared down the creature's throat. Then the shark bit down on Rodney's chest and back.

Rodney struggled to get free. He hit the shark with his fist. But the shark held tight and shook him back and forth.

Then Rodney remembered the weakest spot on a shark's body—its eyes. With all his strength he rammed his right fist straight into the shark's eye. Incredibly, the shark let go.

Bleeding and running out of air, Rodney struggled toward the surface. Could he make it to safety before the great white shark ate him alive?

Rodney reached the surface and gasped for air. He'd made it! But then he looked down. The shark was racing straight for him. Its huge jaws, lined with razor-sharp teeth, were wide open!

SNAP! The shark's jaws slammed shut again. But this time the shark swallowed the fish attached to Rodney's dive belt. Suddenly, Rodney felt himself being pulled through the water—he was still attached to the line!

The shark began to drag him down into deep water. He struggled to undo his dive belt, but the buckle had slipped around his back. He couldn't reach it.

Time was running out. If the shark didn't eat him, Rodney would drown.

Suddenly the line snapped. Rodney was free! He struggled to the surface and shouted for help. Luckily, friends in a nearby boat had seen the blood and quickly pulled him out of the water.

Rodney was seriously hurt. His rib cage, lungs, and the upper part of his

Rodney Fox is one of the few people to have survived the bite of a great white shark.

stomach lay open from the huge gash where the shark had sunk its teeth in. The bite had crushed his ribs and punctured one of his lungs.

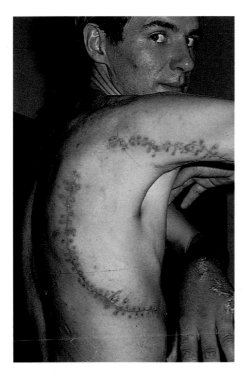

Rodney was rushed to the hospital. Four hours of surgery and 462 stitches saved his life. But he would wear the ugly scar of the shark's bite forever.

The attack on Rodney was big news. The public, frightened of more attacks, demanded action to clear the local beaches of sharks. But Rodney thought differently.

Rodney didn't want to go out and kill sharks—he wanted to go out and learn more about the mysterious creature that had nearly killed him. And he began a lifelong search to find out more about these silent hunters of the deep.

Only a few months after the attack, Rodney was diving again. So he could study sharks up close, Rodney designed and built the first shark cage.

Rodney Fox still dives with sharks, and is now trying to save them from extinction.

A shark cage is about the size of a small elevator car. It is made of very strong metal bars, which are placed close enough together to keep a shark from biting the divers inside but still allow the divers a good view of the shark. Floats at the top keep the cage from sinking.

Today many people use shark cages. They allow divers and scientists to study and photograph sharks up close—but not quite as close as Rodney once came!

Experience the adventure of a lifetime.

GREAT WHITE SHARK
adventure

You'll be guided by dive instructors and shark research experts to see the great white shark in its natural habitat.

Inside the diving cage, you will be safe and secure and still feel the thrill of experiencing what it is like to swim with sharks. You can move around comfortably with all-around view.

Diving safely to see the sharks prevents shark fishing in the area. By supporting us, you are helping us protect sharks and their habitat.

Rule
Must be age 18 or older to dive with the sharks!

Shark Attacks—The Facts

If you're terrified of sharks, you're not alone. Shark attacks make frightening headlines, and movies like *Jaws* spread the fear that sharks are bloodthirsty killers. In fact, many people are scared just by the thought of sharks.

But the truth is that shark attacks are actually very rare. A person is far more likely to be hit by a car or struck by lightning than be attacked by a shark.

Popular fiction has helped spread false fears about sharks.

There are more than 350 different species—or types—of sharks. And of these, only about 30 have ever been known to attack humans. But there are three that are really dangerous: the great white shark, the bull shark, and the tiger shark.

A tiger shark is large and powerful enough to attack most sea creatures.

Bull sharks are one of the few sharks that can live in both fresh and sea water.

The great white shark is the most feared and fearsome of all sharks. It has even been known to attack boats.

Whether or not you are in danger of a shark attack depends on where you live in the world. Sharks are found almost everywhere, but they seem to prefer warm water. Most shark attacks happen in Australia, Brazil, California, Florida, Hawaii, and South Africa. They often occur near crowded beaches where people go to swim, sail, and surf.

◆ *This symbol on the map shows the location of fatal shark attacks around the world.*

But even in a very bad year, sharks attack no more than 80 to 100 people in the whole world. And modern transportation and medical care mean that only 10 to 15 of these people die.

Even then, sharks don't usually set out to attack people. Often they ignore people in the water. So what makes a shark attack a human?

Some people believe sharks attack when they feel threatened. A diver may unknowingly swim into a shark's territory. In this case, a shark may only bite a human once. It will then release—rather than eat—the invader.

Perhaps this is what happened to diver Henry Bource. A single bite from a large shark resulted in him losing a leg.

Divers are sometimes attacked while carrying fish they have caught. The blood and frantic movements of the dying fish attract sharks, who can smell blood from a great distance.

Henry Bource

A shark's view of a seal and a bodyboarder from below

Sometimes a shark attack could be a case of mistaken identity. From a shark's point of view, a surfer or bodyboarder looks like its favorite food—a seal. Once the shark has a taste of the board, it will spit it out and go away. Many surfers are still alive to tell the tale, with a munched surfboard to prove it!

This surfer's board was bitten by a 13-foot (4-meter) tiger shark in Hawaii.

An attack may happen because a shark is very hungry. Experts think that Raymond Short was attacked by a hungry shark while swimming in the water off a crowded Australian beach.

Raymond was swimming near the shore when he was bitten by a shark. Six lifeguards immediately dashed into the sea to save him. But as they started to carry Raymond toward the shore, the lifeguards realized the shark was still attached to Raymond's leg!

Raymond had to be
pulled right onto
the beach before
the shark let
go of his leg.

The shark had a long wound along
its stomach. It had been badly injured.
Scientists think the shark had been
unable to catch its normal food and
was so hungry it took unusual risks.

Another strange attack took place in a very unexpected place—a creek!

Twelve-year-old Lester Stillwell was swimming with his friends in Matawan Creek in New Jersey. Suddenly, he screamed and disappeared beneath the water. A man named Stanley Fisher rushed into the creek to drag Lester's lifeless body from the water. Suddenly, Stanley felt something bump his right leg. When he reached down, he realized part of his leg had been ripped away.

They had been attacked by a shark! Tragically, both died from their wounds.

Was this attack really so strange? Not if you know about sharks. Even though the shark was never found, it was most likely a bull shark, a species that lives in both salt and fresh water.

Deadliest Sharks

Great white shark

🔖 **Length** up to 20 ft (6 m)

⚖️ **Weight** up to 4,400 lb (2,000 kgs)

Largest of the predatory sharks, the great white has 300 sawlike teeth. Its jutting upper jaw helps it grab chunks of meat off its prey. It's responsible for most shark attacks on humans.

Hammerhead shark

🔖 **Length** up to 20 ft (6 m)

⚖️ **Weight** up to 1,000 lb (450 kgs)

The widely spaced eyes and nostrils of a hammerhead shark help it pinpoint its prey's exact location. If a hammerhead wants you, it will find you!

Tiger shark

Length up to 15 ft (4.25 m)
Weight up to 1,400 lb (635 kgs)

This shark has sharp teeth and powerful jaws that can chomp through a sea turtle's shell. It will eat anything from seals and dolphins to floating junk such as tin cans.

Bull shark

Length up to 11.5 ft (3.4 m)
Weight up to 500 lb (230 kgs)

A bull shark uses its body weight to attack by bumping its prey first and then going in for the big bite! It can swim far up into rivers and even enter lakes.

Sharks and Safety

People have tried many ways to protect themselves from shark attacks as they explore the shark's watery world.

One of the most popular methods of protecting swimmers is simply to build a fence, or shark net, in the water. These shark nets are used off many popular Australian and South African beaches.

Shark nets are set up off popular beaches.

Nets stop sharks from swimming into an area.

But the nets cost a lot of money to build and often need repair.

Electrical beach barriers are also being tested, since sharks won't swim through strong electric currents.

A big problem with shark nets is that they trap and kill all types of sharks, as well as other creatures like dolphins.

How to avoid a shark attack:

- Never swim by yourself.
- Don't swim if you have a cut. Sharks can smell blood a mile (1.6 km) away.
- Don't swim at dusk, as this is the time when sharks are likely to be feeding.
- Don't urinate in the ocean. Sharks are attracted to the smell.
- Get out of the water if a shark is seen in the ocean.

People who are victims of shipwrecks or plane crashes at sea are often at risk of being attacked by a shark because they are so far from land.

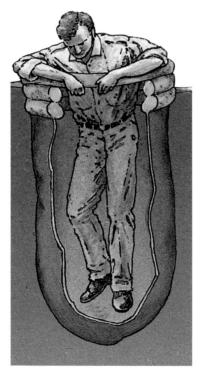

One invention to protect people floating in the sea is the shark screen bag. It is like a large plastic bag, which is closed at the bottom and has floats at the top. When not in use, it is small enough to be folded up and tucked into a pocket. But when inflated, the bag hides the person's shape, movement, smells, and sounds from passing sharks, hopefully keeping the person safe until help arrives.

Many people have tried to invent a chemical shark repellent. During World War II, many soldiers were killed by sharks when their ships sank. The army tried to make a repellent made of chemicals and dye. It was meant to repel sharks and hide the person from the shark. But it didn't work because it melted too quickly.

One of the latest ideas is to try to copy the poison made by a fish called the Moses sole. If caught by a shark, the fish squirts out poison. Sharks hate the taste so much, they spit the fish out!

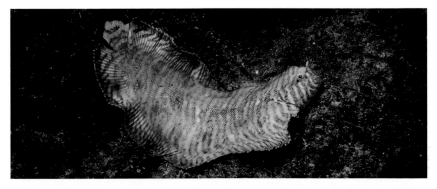

A Moses sole swims very slowly and protects itself with poison.

Divers who dive for sport or to study and film underwater life often come face to face with dangerous sharks. Some carry spear guns, or bangsticks that fire a small explosive charge that can kill a shark. But for those who want to study sharks, killing them is not the answer.

A bangstick is more effective than a spear gun against a large shark.

Valerie and Ron Taylor developed a new idea. These Australian filmmakers are well known for their underwater photography. But it is dangerous work. Valerie has the shark bites to prove it!

On one dive trip, the Taylors noticed a crew member wearing some stainless steel mesh gloves to protect his hands while cleaning fish. This gave them an idea. Why not make a whole dive suit out of chain mail to protect divers from sharks—like the chain mail suits worn by knights?

They made a suit out of 400,000 tiny stainless steel rings. But to test the suit, someone had to wear it in the water. Someone had to make the sharks bite!

Valerie in her chain mail suit

The Taylors carried out a test dive off the coast of California. Raw chunks of fish were dumped into the water to attract sharks. Valerie Taylor zipped up the chain mail suit over her regular dive suit and then dived into the water among the raw chunks of fish.

Soon several sharks darted in. Valerie waved a bleeding fish close to her body, baiting the sharks to bite. Suddenly, a shark chomped down on Valerie's arm! She was startled, but not hurt.

The shark bit her again and again all over her body. It was frightening, but the shark's teeth couldn't get through the mesh. The suit had worked!

But it wasn't all so easy. At one point, a shark pulled off one of Valerie's gloves and bit her thumb. Valerie managed to fight off the shark and get away to safety.

The suit needed small improvements. But thanks to Valerie's bravery, the first practical shark suit had been invented!

Diver protected from a shark attack by his chain mail suit

Why We Need Sharks

Sharks are important because they are at the top of the oceanic food chain. They keep ocean life healthy and balanced.

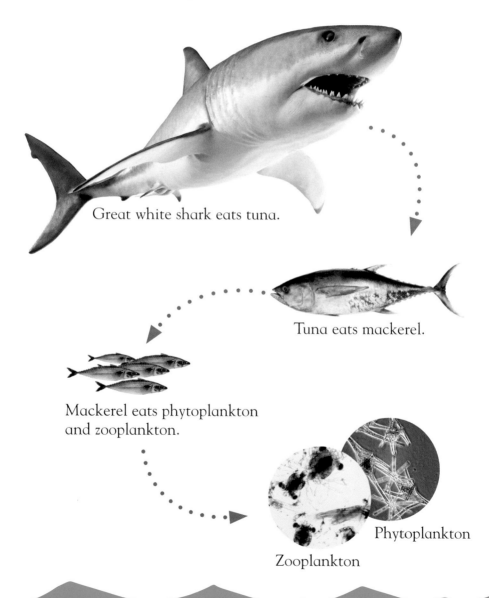

Great white shark eats tuna.

Tuna eats mackerel.

Mackerel eats phytoplankton and zooplankton.

Phytoplankton

Zooplankton

As the top predator, sharks control the population of fish lower in the food chain.

Sharks mostly prey on old, sick, and weak fish, so the fitter fish live on to pass their healthy qualities to their babies.

Sharks hunt smaller fish that might otherwise eat too much phytoplankton. Phytoplankton are ocean plants, which produce oxygen that is needed for ocean life to flourish.

The survival of ocean creatures and their habitats depends on the shark population of the region.

Sharks Up Close

Sharks have roamed the Earth's oceans for nearly 400 million years and are 200 million years older than the dinosaurs! But today's sharks are a lot like their early ancestors.

The biggest of these ancient sharks was called the *Carcharodon megalodon* [car-CARE-oh-don MEG-a-loh-don]. This shark's huge jaws were over 6 feet (1.8 meters) wide. It weighed up to 10,000 pounds (4,535 kilograms) and grew to 54 feet (16 meters). That's twice as long as today's great white shark.

Those early sharks died out. But life in the sea has changed very little, and today's sharks can tell us a lot about the animals that lived millions of years ago.

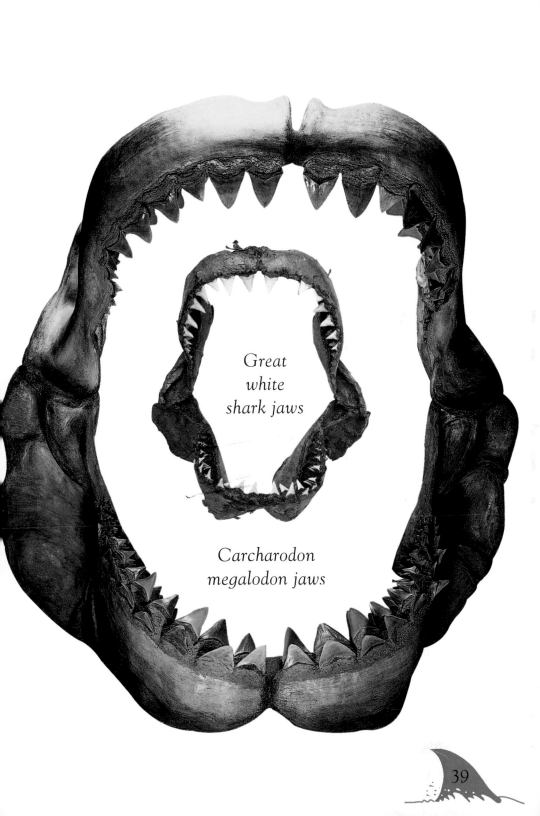

Great
white
shark jaws

Carcharodon
megalodon jaws

The shark is perfectly evolved for surviving and hunting underwater. Its amazingly flexible body is due to a skeleton made of cartilage—the same material that forms our noses and ears!

A shark has the same five senses as a human—sight, hearing, smell, taste, and touch. But the shark's ability to catch prey in murky waters is due to two extra, and very unusual, senses.

The dorsal fin helps balance and steering.

The caudal fin keeps the shark from rolling over.

Pectoral fins act as brakes.

Gills take oxygen from the water.

The "lateral line" is a series of invisible pressure-sensitive organs on each side of a shark's body. These help the shark sense very small vibrations in the water.

On the head of a shark are tiny pores called the ampullae of Lorenzini [am-POOL-ee of lor-un-ZEE-nee]. They allow a shark to sense the faint electrical charges given off by all living things.

Sharks can hear up to 1,000 feet (305 meters).

Ampullae of Lorenzini

Sharks can see up to 50 feet (15 meters) away.

Sharks are solitary animals—they live, swim, and hunt alone. Scientists know very little about their life cycle. What is known, however, is that sharks are very slow to reproduce. Some sharks take 11 years before they are ready to mate. When sharks do give birth, they often have few babies, so they take extra care to protect their eggs. Many sharks

Egg cases

lay their eggs in tough protective egg cases. Other sharks give birth to live babies called pups. These pups are already quite big when they are born, which helps them survive.

Shark pups

Sharks eat most kinds of food—but all sharks eat meat. Many eat small fish and animals

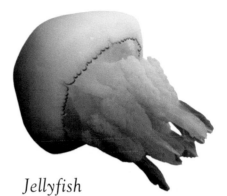

Jellyfish

like jellyfish and lobsters, although tin cans and plastic bags have also been found in a shark's stomach! Some larger sharks hunt bigger animals, such as seals, penguins, and even other sharks. A few, like the basking shark, simply swim along with their mouths wide open. They catch plankton, the tiny plant and animal life in the ocean, as well as small animals such as shrimp.

Seals

43

Do you think you know what a shark looks like? Maybe you should think again! When most people think of sharks, they imagine the great white. But sharks come in all sizes and some very unusual shapes. Just look at the angel shark, the horn shark, the hammerhead shark, and the wobbegong!

Hammerhead shark

Lantern shark

Angel shark

The biggest shark is the whale shark. It can grow up to 40 feet (12.2 meters) long and weigh as much as 13 tons (13.2 metric tons), making it the largest fish in the world. One of the smallest sharks is the lantern shark. It only grows to 8 inches (20 centimeters) long! It is known as the lantern shark because its eyes glow in the dark!

Horn shark

Wobbegong shark

Whale shark

Tagging Sharks

By Melanie Sharp

Sharks are amazing creatures. Sadly, many species of shark are also endangered, so scientists must take great care when studying them.

Sharks swim too fast and too deep for people to follow them. So scientists tag the sharks to track their movements. Tagging can tell us about a shark's size, swimming speed, movement patterns in the ocean, body temperature, and depth in the water.

As the number of shark conservation projects increases, tagging is helping scientists to discover new information about these fascinating creatures.

How tagging works

1. Scientists attract a shark to their boat by using dead fish or fish oil as bait.

2. As the shark takes the bait, scientists carefully pull the shark into the boat.

3. Scientists keep the shark in a tub of water to weigh and measure it.

Scientists attach a tag to the dorsal fin of a hammerhead shark

4. Scientists then attach a tag to the shark's dorsal fin and release it back into the water.

5. After a while, the tag automatically detaches from the shark's body and floats to the surface of the water. Scientists then collect the tag.

Sometimes, divers use tagging poles to tag sharks in the water

Sharks Under Attack

For centuries people have feared sharks. But, today, sharks have much more to fear from people. Overfishing is threatening many species with extinction.

Shark's tooth necklace

Sharks have been hunted for many years. Their flesh and teeth were used for weapons, food, and even jewelry. But the numbers caught posed no threat to the shark population.

Today, modern fishing methods mean that sharks are killed in huge numbers—up to 100 million sharks each year. As a result, the population of some shark species may have dropped by as much as 80 percent in the last ten years.

Often the sharks are killed by accident because they get trapped in fishing nets. The fishermen keep the fish they want and throw the unwanted sharks back into the ocean—dead.

Much shark killing is just for sport. People who hunt and kill a shark may seem brave, but they are never in any danger. The jaws make flashy trophies that sell to tourists for lots of money.

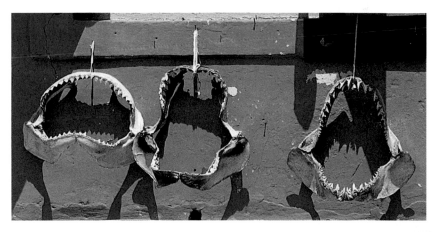

This shark hunter hangs his victims' jaws around his boat.

49

Shark meal

Sharks are also under attack because, in many parts of the world, people eat shark meat. In Asia, shark-fin soup is an expensive treat. Some fishermen earn so much money from shark fins that, when they catch a shark, they hack off its fins and throw the dying animal back into the water.

Fins from any type of shark are used to make shark-fin soup.

In some countries shark cartilage is made into health pills. Some people believe that the pills will cure almost anything, from heart disease to cancer. Nearly all of these claims are false.

Shark skin is also tanned and made into very expensive leather belts and wallets.

One of the most valuable shark products is

Modern shark leather box

its liver. The oil taken from a shark's liver is used in many products, including industrial oils and medicines. The oil was also used to make vitamin A pills until the 1950s when a different source was found.

Vitamin A tablets

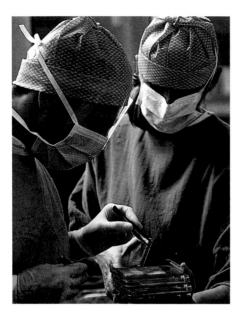

Doctors with artificial skin grown from shark cartilage

If we don't control the mass killing of sharks, they may become extinct. But why would this matter?

Scientists have discovered many amazing things about sharks, and we have a great deal to learn from this ancient creature. Sharks may even save our lives one day.

For instance, researchers have found that squalene, a chemical found in the liver and stomach of the dogfish shark, slows down the growth of tumors in people. Shark cartilage is also now used to make artificial skin for burn patients.

Sharks have highly developed immune systems, too—which means they don't often get sick. Their cuts and wounds heal very fast. They rarely get cancer like some animals can, even when scientists inject cancer cells into the sharks' bodies in the laboratory.

Why? Scientists don't know yet, but studying sharks may help doctors cure people who are sick.

This great white shark has been cut by struggling prey, but the wounds will soon heal.

Aquariums are safe places to go and see a shark!

The more we learn about sharks, the more we will learn to admire and respect them. Of course most people don't want to come face to face with a great white shark in the ocean—like Rodney Fox!

But we can visit sharks in aquariums and watch fascinating films made by underwater filmmakers. We can even take trips to see sharks in the sea.

Sharks are fascinating, intelligent, and graceful creatures. Only a few kinds of sharks are dangerous. Attacks on people are really very rare. The shark's reputation as a bloodthirsty killer is not accurate or fair.

Sharks have had a home on our planet far longer than we have. It would be a shame if people made them disappear from our seas forever.

The Myth
of
THE SHARK PRINCE

Long, long ago, the prince of sharks lived on the island of Hawaii. His name was Nanave. He had a human body, but on his back was the mouth of a great white shark. He always wore a feathered cape to hide it. The cape was the only thing his father, the king of sharks, had left him before returning to the sea.

With the cape safely covering his back, Nanave would ask passing fishermen in the village where to find the best catch. The unsuspecting fishermen readily told him. Soon however, they found the size of their catch getting smaller and smaller. What was happening to all the fish?

One day, when Nanave was in the village, the chief asked each person to run over a trail of leaves to find out who was scaring the fish away. Nanave knew that only human feet would leave impressions in the leaves. When it was his turn, the frightened Nanave ran over the leaves, but his cape slipped away to reveal the shark mouth on his back!

Seeing this, the angry villagers chased Nanave.
He escaped into a natural pool that led to the sea.
As he dove into the water, he turned into a shark and
the villagers threw big rocks at him. When the pool
filled up with rocks, they thought they had killed him.

However, Nanave found a tunnel his father had
made to lead him to the sea. Soon, father and son
were reunited and never returned to the village
again. Since that day, the fishermen never reveal
where they are going to fish, for fear that a shark
in disguise might hear them!

Amazing Facts

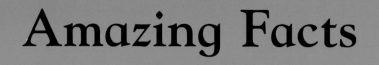

A shark never runs out of teeth. When one tooth falls out, another takes its place. Many sharks lose between 8,000 and 20,000 teeth in a lifetime.

Most sharks are fussy eaters. If they don't like the taste of their first bite, they will spit it out and move on!

Sharks are the biggest fish in the sea! Whale sharks can reach up to 40 ft (12.2 m), which is longer than a bus.

Sharks have extremely stretchy stomachs. They can live off one giant meal for several days.

Sharks are super smart! They have been known to plan their attacks and sneak up on their prey from behind.

Shark Quiz

1. What did Rodney Fox design and build to help him study sharks safely?

2. What time of day are sharks most likely to be feeding?

3. Who tested the first chain mail suit designed to protect divers from shark attacks?

4. What was the biggest of the ancient sharks called?

5. What is the name of the fin that helps sharks balance and steer in water?

Answers on page 61.

Glossary

Ampullae of Lorenzini
[am-POOL-ee of lor-un-ZEE-nee]
Tiny pores on a shark's head that can detect faint electrical signals in the water.

Aquarium
A large tank where sea animals are kept so people can view them safely.

Bangstick
An underwater gun that fires a small explosive charge that is strong enough to kill a large shark.

Carcharodon megalodon
[car-CARE-oh-don MEG-a-loh-don]
The largest shark that ever lived in the sea. It died out over 10 million years ago.

Cartilage
A tough, flexible material from which a shark's skeleton is made. Human noses and ears are also made of cartilage.

Chain mail suit
A dive suit made up of thousands of tiny interlocking stainless steel rings. It protects divers from shark bites.

Extinction
When a particular animal or plant dies out completely.

Fossils
The remains of plants and animals that lived millions of years ago. Fossils are often in rocks.

Lateral line
A line of invisible points on each side of a shark's body that help sharks sense vibrations in the water.

Moses sole
A slow fish that releases a poisonous liquid when caught.

Plankton
Tiny animals and plants that live in the sea.

Shark cage
A small metal cage that protects divers.

Shark repellent
A mix of chemicals and dye shaped into a cake. It was meant to protect people from sharks.

Shark net
A net that is hung under the water to stop sharks from reaching swimmers off a beach.

Shark screen bag
An inflatable bag that hides shipwreck victims from sharks by hiding any smells or movements.

Spearfishing
Fishing underwater with a spear gun.

Spear gun
An underwater gun that fires spears. It is used by underwater divers to catch fish.

Squalene
A valuable chemical found in a shark's liver. Humans use it for a number of medical reasons.

Index

Answers to the Shark Quiz:

1. A shark cage; **2.** At dusk; **3.** Valerie Taylor;
4. *Carcharodon megalodon*; **5.** Dorsal fin.

Guide for Parents

DK Readers is a four-level interactive reading adventure series for children, developing the habit of reading widely for both pleasure and information. These books have an exciting main narrative interspersed with a range of reading genres to suit your child's reading ability, as required by the Common Core State Standards. Each book is designed to develop your child's reading skills, fluency, grammar awareness, and comprehension in order to build confidence and engagement when reading.

Ready for a *Reading Alone* book

YOUR CHILD SHOULD

- be able to read most words without needing to stop and break them down into sound parts.
- read smoothly, in phrases and with expression. By this level, your child will be mostly reading silently.
- self-correct when some word or sentence doesn't sound right.

A VALUABLE AND SHARED READING EXPERIENCE

For some children, text reading, particularly nonfiction, requires much effort, but adult participation can make this both fun and easier. So here are a few tips on how to use this book with your child.

TIP 1 Check out the contents together before your child begins:

- invite your child to check the blurb, contents page, and layout of the book and comment on it.
- ask your child to make predictions about the story.
- talk about the information your child might want to find out.

TIP 2 Encourage fluent and flexible reading:

- support your child to read in fluent, expressive phrases, making full use of punctuation and thinking about the meaning.

- encourage your child to slow down and check information where appropriate.

TIP 3 **Indicators that your child is reading for meaning:**

- your child will be responding to the text if he/she is self-correcting and varying his/her voice.

- your child will want to talk about what he/she is reading or is eager to turn the page to find out what will happen next.

TIP 4 **Share and discuss:**

- encourage your child to recall specific details after each chapter.

- provide opportunities for your child to pick out interesting words and discuss what they mean.

- discuss how the author captures the reader's interest, or how effective the nonfiction layouts are.

- ask questions about the text. These help to develop comprehension skills and awareness of the language used.

A FEW ADDITIONAL TIPS

- Read to your child regularly to demonstrate fluency, phrasing, and expression; to find out or check information; and for sharing enjoyment.

- Encourage your child to reread favorite texts to increase reading confidence and fluency.

- Check that your child is reading a range of different types of material, such as poems, jokes, and following instructions.

Series consultant, **Dr. Linda Gambrell**, Distinguished Professor of Education at Clemson University, has served as President of the National Reading Conference, the College Reading Association, and the International Reading Association. She is also reading consultant for the **DK Adventures**.

Have you read these other great books from DK?

Meet the sharks who live on the reef or come passing through.

Join David on an amazing trip to meet elephants in Asia and Africa.

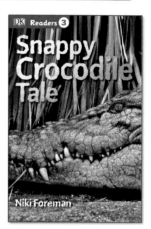

Follow Chris Croc's adventures from a baby to a mighty king of the river.

Discover what it takes to become a first-rate player with soccer skills, tips, and tactics.

Design and test a rocket for a spying mission. Try out some experiments at home.

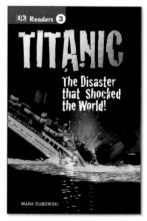

This is the incredible true story of the "unsinkable" ship that sank.